THE
LOON SPIRIT

BY PHIL HARPER
ILLUSTRATIONS BY MARK COYLE

NorthWord
PRESS, INC

Minocqua, Wisconsin

FOR STEVE AND OTHER PILGRIMS
TO THE BOUNDARY WATERS

NorthWord Press, Inc.
P.O. Box 1360
Minocqua, WI 54548

Designed by Russell S. Kuepper

For a free catalog describing NorthWord's
line of nature books and gifts, call 1-800-336-5666.

ISBN 1-55971-463-8

Library of Congress Cataloging-in-Publication Data

Harper, Phil
    The Loon Spirit / by Phil Harper ; illustrations by Mark Coyle.
        p. cm.
    Summary: As the Loon Spirit heralds each change of the season
in the great north woods, the animals and plants respond to his call.
    ISBN 1-55971-463-8
    [1. Seasons—Fiction. 2. Nature—Fiction.] I. Coyle, Mark ill.
II. Title.
PZ7.H2317Lo 1995
    [Fic]—dc20   94-24958
                                                            CIP
                                                             AC

Printed in Mexico.

THE
LOON SPIRIT

BY PHIL HARPER

ILLUSTRATIONS BY MARK COYLE

Deep in the great north woods, upon an island in the land of many waters, rests a figure in the softness of a winter's snow.

It is Lakucha, the Loon Spirit. Safe beneath the figure's folded wings lies the warmth of many summers.

When winter's long nights have passed and the howling winds have blown away, the sun's return awakens Lakucha, calling the spirit from far off realms.

Slowly the figure arises. The great beaked head, like some ancient enchanted mask, gazes across the frozen waters. The feathered limbs stretch forth in awakening. The long robe shimmers like midnight waters beneath the moon. With a shake, Lakucha ruffles the shimmering feathers. From the great beak, the Loon Spirit's long cry reaches out across the frozen waters.

Karoooooo!
Karoooooo!
Karoooooo!

It echoes through the great wilderness. The snow-covered waters answer with resounding cracks, heralding the coming of spring.

Slowly Lakucha's wings unfurl. Their mighty sweep clears the snows from across the awakening land.

With the beat of powerful wings, Lakucha rises to the winds. The warmth of life flows forth as the Loon Spirit soars over the land of many waters.

Spring returns.

The squirrels call to Lakucha with their chittering.

The trees return to greening, heeding the awakening call with the soft rustle of newborn leaves.

The great bears lumber out of their deep shelters.

A few grateful deer munch the delicate grasses in the warm returning sunlight.

The first brave
wildflowers peek
their heads up
through the
thawing earth.

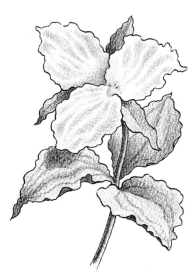

Life comes again to the land of many waters.

The task is done.
The land has awakened
again. Transforming
into a common loon,
Lakucha rests upon the
waters. Only the flecks
of starlight in its eyes
betray the Loon Spirit's
presence.

Through the cricketing
summer Lakucha floats,
keeping watch over the land.

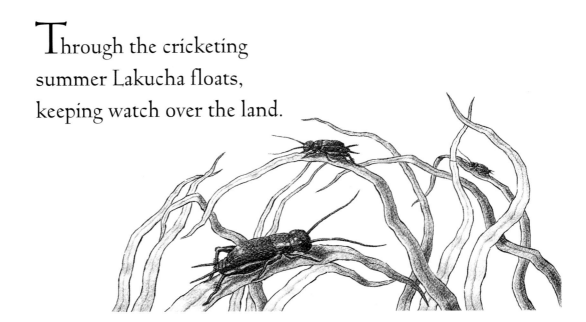

Over high cliffs, the solitary eagles soar.

Along the shoreline, great bears trudge.

Fish leap, splashing in the clear water.

Gentle rains sweep the faces of the many waters
with their myriad pitter patters.

In the evenings, quiet deer come
to drink by the lapping shore.

A cautious wolf sniffs the telltale breeze.

A solitary loon calls.

Lakucha answers with the cry of life.

Karoooooo!
Karoooooo!
Karoooooo!

Yet when summer's warmth fades and the nights return to coolness, Lakucha's true form is again called forth. Transforming again, the mighty figure spreads its wings and soars, calling to the trees.

Karoooooo!
Karoooooo!
Karoooooo!

With flames of colors they answer.

The summer flowers fall asleep in the fields,
dreaming of rebirth.

The squirrels heed the cry
as they store their winter nuts.

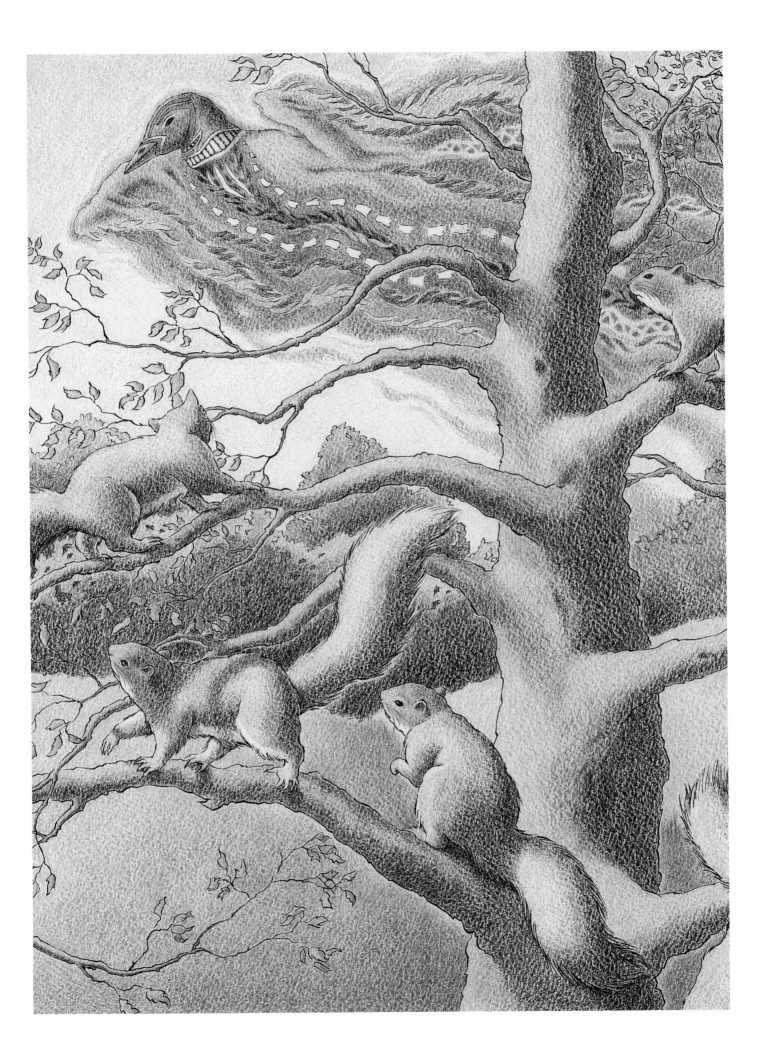

The great bears yawn and
search for deep shelter.

With a graceful sweep of wings,
Lakucha once again gathers in the life-giving warmth.

With the season's turning,
the Loon Spirit returns to the island refuge.

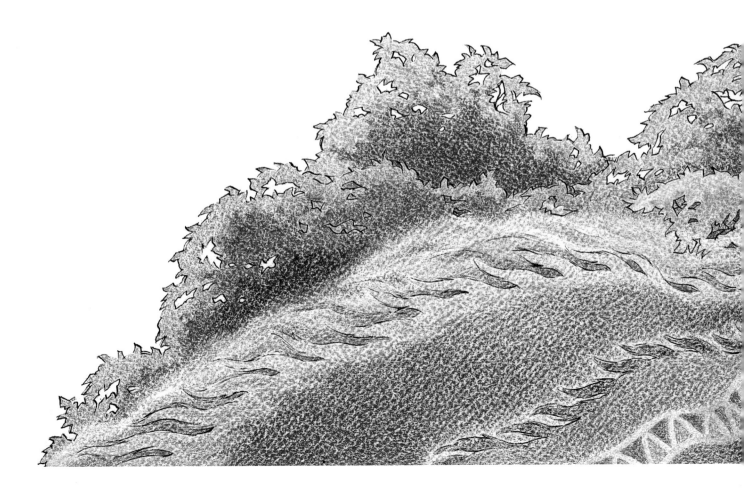

The great wings are folded. The dark-robed body settles. The summer's warmth of life lies safe within its feathered form.

As the bears fall to sleep, and the loons fly south, the great beaked head is tucked beneath the wings and Lakucha rests, flying to other realms on invisible wings.

Soon, all around is gentle crystal, white with the first snows of winter. The wild places echo with the sounds of the deep silence.

Lakucha, the keeper of that sacred
land, waits again for spring.